CURATION-TEMPLATES

Britt Malka

To receive emails with information about new books, offers and more, please sign up at
http://brittmalka.com/non-fiction/
for my non-fiction books.

Britt Malka has been utilizing curation since 2003, long before the concept became at all popular. In this Kindle book, she shares five templates that make it easy to create evergreen curated blog posts, even though you may be lacking inspiration and suffering from writer's block.

You'll also receive a short introduction to curation, as well as how to use the templates.

By obtaining this book, you'll be on your way to creating valuable blog content that will stay evergreen for years.

Chapter 1 - Introduction to Curation

Hi!

I'm Britt Malka, and I've been implementing curation since May 2003. At that time, I didn't realize I was actually doing curation, because the use of this fancy word wasn't as yet linked to acquiring this type of content.

There are many informative books and video courses about curation in the marketplace, so the goal of this book is not to teach you about curation as such, but rather to help you curate blog posts as quickly, effectively and competently as possible.

However, just to make sure that we're both on the same page, I'll give you a short introduction to curation, such as I see it.

Curation - in short - is finding the 'best of the best' content, and then delivering it to your readers.

You can compare curation to the work of a grand chef in a highly-priced five star restaurant.

He chooses the best raw ingredients, then cooks and arranges them in order to offer a tasty and unforgettable experience for his guests.

You should be doing the same thing, when you curate content. It's not simply just a case of finding existing material using a keyword, then copying and pasting the complete thing onto your blog. Your readers are fully capable of using a search engine themselves.

No, you should only choose the best ingredients and serve them, garnished with your knowledge and spiced with your personal experience. That's how you turn good raw ingredients into a delicious dish, one that would have your readers salivating at the result.

How do you find the 'crème de la crème' to share with your readers?

By following authority blogs in your niche, and also by choosing pertinent comments from knowledgeable writers in relevant forums. Now that you know where to go to find suitable content, you can then use your keywords to search for bites from within these authority blogs and forum writers to feature in your curated blog posts.

Chapter 2 - How to Use Templates

If you stumble upon a blog post on an authority blog, and the content inspires you to write your own blog post, you probably don't need a template. You can just create your own headline; write an introduction; quote what is necessary; give credits to the original blog post – and, finally, write your own comments below.

This is curation in its simplest form.

But if you want to run a successful blog, you need to frequently add new content. Daily is best, but then you'll probably run out of ideas once in a while.

This is where templates come into the picture.

When you're struggling to find a subject about which to write a blog post, choose a template, and then use this as your guide. You'll be almost 100% guaranteed to come up with a blog post, just based on using that template alone.

In this book, I'll give you five templates to use to assist you in writing evergreen blog posts.

And, in the last chapter, you'll find a link to a PDF file with actual examples of how to use the five templates. I chose not to include the examples in this Kindle book, because you need to see the format of the blog posts; where something is quoted; pictures and videos etc.

If you have any questions, feel free to contact me and ask. You can write to me here:

britt@malka.biz

Good luck with your curation work!

Britt Malka

CHAPTER 3 - THE 'TOP TEN' CURATION TEMPLATE

'Top Tens' are always popular amongst readers, but it can be time consuming to write them all yourself.

With curation, writing a full length blog post around this idea becomes a breeze.

If your items are lengthy enough, you can use less than ten; for example: 'Top Three', 'Top Five', or 'Top Seven'.

This is how you use the template:

1: Create a list of ten things in your niche. It could be the top ten Android apps, or the top ten authority sites, or any other related subject.

2: Find texts or videos that expand on each of your ten points.

3: Create an attention-grabbing headline for your blog post. If possible, use keywords, together with the words 'Top Ten', to arouse curiosity.

4: Write an introduction to your blog post.

5: List your ten things. Use each thing as a sub-head, or format these words in bold.

6: Write why you think this item belongs on your top ten, and use a quote from an authority site, or embed a video, to further confirm your choice. Remember to add a link back to the source.

7: Do this for each of your ten things.

8: Write an outro (ending, conclusion, finish) to your blog post.

CHAPTER 4 - THE 'SEVEN TIPS' CURATION TEMPLATE

People love tips. Tips are often short reads that are easy to implement, and when you offer your readers a suitable number of tips, they are bound to read your list.

You can use three, five, seven or ten tips. Personally, I prefer seven.

This is how to use the template:

1: Think of seven tips that you'd like to share regarding your niche.

2: Do some research and find texts, videos and/or pictures that support your tips.

3: Create an intriguing headline which includes the words 'Seven Tips'.

4: Write an introduction to your blog post.

5: List your seven tips, and use each of them as a sub-head, or format them in bold type.

6: Quote any text you've found, or embed a picture or video that explains how to use your tip. Remember to link back to the source. Add your own comments to further improve the tip.

7: Write an outro to your blog post.

CHAPTER 5 - THE 'X REASONS WHY' CURATION TEMPLATE

Give your readers reasons whereby your particular take on a subject is valid, and substantiate it with texts, pictures or videos that you find on other websites.

You can use this template to write blog posts such as 'Five Reasons Why a Kindle is Better than an iPad'; or 'Seven Reasons Why You Should Outsource Your Work'; or anything else you wish to write and share with your readers.

Use the template like this:

1: Think of a topic that is 'in' at the moment within your

niche.

2: Take a defined stand on your opinion, and write a list of reasons to support it.

3: Find blog texts, articles, forum posts, videos and/pictures that support your reasons as to why you took this approach.

4: Create a controversial, funny (or in other ways) attention-grabbing headline.

5: Write an introduction to your blog post.

6: List your reasons, and make each reason stand out by making it a sub-head, or format it in bold type.

7: Post text excerpts, videos or pictures to illustrate each reason. Link back to the sources, and add your own comments.

8: Write an outro to your blog post.

CHAPTER 6 - THE PROS AND CONS CURATION TEMPLATE

When you write this particular type of curated blog post, you're not only showing your expertise, but simultaneously saving yourself time.

The basic idea is that you take a stand on a topic that is being debated within your niche. You then show both sides of the argument - those that are *for* (the pros) and those that are *against* (the cons). Finally, add your own comments.

1: Take a stand on a debated topic. Are you for, or against it?

2: Find texts, videos, podcasts, PDF's or anything else that illustrates the view point of somebody who is for the debated topic.

3: Find texts, videos, podcasts, PDF's or anything that supports the view point of somebody who is against the debated topic.

4: Create a controversial, funny (or in any other way) attention- grabbing headline.

5: Write an introduction to your blog post.

6: Make a sub-head for the view point of your topic.

7: Write an introduction to the *for* point of view, and add quotes, pictures or videos to support this view. Give credit to the sources by linking back to them.

8: You can add your own comments at this point of time, or wait until you complete the copy.

9: Use the same procedure for the *against* point of view.

10: Add your comments at the end of the blog post. Where do you stand - and why?

11: Write an outro to your blog post.

CHAPTER 7 - THE 'FAQ' CURATION TEMPLATE

Using the FAQ format always makes it quick and fun to write a blog post. Now, when you add curation to the equation, it becomes even more simple and enjoyable.

You can use the template this way:

1: Choose your topic, and find a number of frequently asked questions relating to it. Feel free to invent your own questions. Or you can take them from emails, forum posts or Yahoo Answers.

2: Create an interesting headline for your blog post.

3: Write an introduction. Let your readers know that you are about to answer some important questions regarding your niche.

4: List your frequently asked questions. Format them so they stand out clearly and legibly.

5: Find answers to each question on YouTube, forums or authority blogs. Quote or embed what is necessary, and add your own take on it. Remember to link back to all the sources in order to give credit where it is due.

6: Write an outro to your blog post.

Chapter 8 - Valuable Resources

As promised, here's the link to the PDF file featuring examples of how to use the five templates:

http://getmoneymakingideas.com/go/5ct/

Inside the above PDF file, read how you can obtain a PDF copy of the templates I've written about in this Kindle-book. You might find it easier to use them by copying them directly from the PDF file to your blog posts. Of course, they are free for you to use.

My Kindle Books:

Check all my books at http://BrittMalka.com